Castles

Jenny Vaughan

Franklin Watts
London   New York   Toronto   Sydney

12688

©1984 Franklin Watts Ltd

First published in Great Britain
    1984 by
Franklin Watts Ltd
12a Golden Square
London W1

First published in the USA by
Franklin Watts Inc.
387 Park Avenue South
New York
N.Y. 10016

UK ISBN: 0 86313 080 1
US ISBN: 0-531-04706-7
Library of Congress Catalog Card
    Number: 83-50592

Printed in Great Britain by
    Cambus Litho, East Kilbride

Designed by
Jim Marks

Edited by
Judith Maxwell

Technical consultant
Brian Davison BA, FSA, MIFA

Photographs supplied by
Wales Tourist Board, ZEFA.
The photograph on page 27 is
Crown Copyright – reproduced
with permission of the Controller
of Her Majesty's Stationery Office.

Illustrated by
Jeff Burn, Simon Evans,
John James/Temple Art.

AN
EASY-READ
FACT
BOOK

Castles

Contents

What is a castle?

▽ This is a wooden castle, known as a motte-and-bailey castle. Many were built in the 11th century. The lower yard or bailey was surrounded by a ditch and a fence called a palisade. A hall, chapel, kitchen and stables stood in the bailey.

A castle was a home that was also a fortress. Castles were built hundreds of years ago by kings and noblemen.

When a king conquered a new land, he had to stop his enemies winning it back. So he gave parts of it to his noblemen. In return, they kept their area safe for the king.

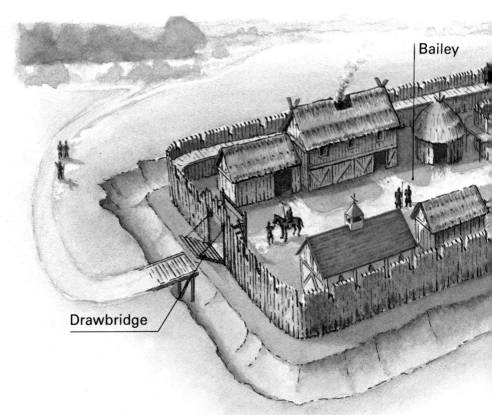

Bailey

Drawbridge

4

Each nobleman had knights to help him. He had to protect his knights and their horses from attack. To do this, the nobleman built a castle.

Because the land was full of enemies, the nobleman had to build his castle quickly. So he built it of wood, for wood was easy to get and cheap, and building with wood was quick.

▽Earth from the ditches was piled up to form a mound or motte. The tower on top of the motte was the safest place in the castle. People hid there if enemy soldiers broke into the bailey.

Tower

Motte

Palisade

Stone castles

Wood is not the best material to use for building because it rots. A wooden castle could also be burned down. Where stone was easily available, it was used instead of wood. In other areas, the wooden castles were strengthened with stone.

A stone wall, or curtain wall, was built around the bailey. Like the palisade, this had a walkway inside and was crenellated. A crenellated wall had regular gaps, called crenels, at the top. Guards standing on the walkway could look out through them. The stones between the gaps, called merlons, often contained loopholes through which arrows could be fired.

Within the curtain wall there was a strong stone tower, called a keep. This was so heavy that it was usually built on hard ground rather than on a motte. Keeps were often very high and some had walls as thick as 20 ft (6 m).

▷ This castle had a curtain wall strengthened with towers. A well-guarded gatehouse stood at the entrance. The keep was in the inner bailey, protected by a second wall and gatehouse.

The lord might have allowed people from the nearby town to shelter in the castle when danger threatened.

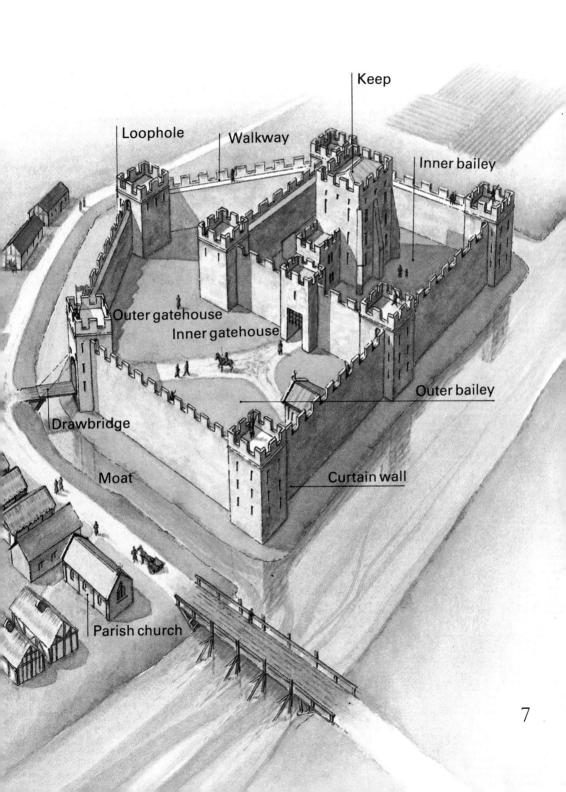

Keep

Loophole Walkway

Inner bailey

Outer gatehouse

Inner gatehouse

Outer bailey

Drawbridge

Moat

Curtain wall

Parish church

7

Inside a castle

The keep was the safest place in the castle. It was also the home of the nobleman and his family.

This keep had three stories. A staircase led up to the well-guarded entrance in the middle story. Here there was a large hall where the lord received visitors and, occasionally, held banquets. Many of his visitors were the people who farmed his lands. He sorted out their problems and settled disputes among them.

The keep also had a room called the solar. This was the family's bedroom and sitting room, and the place where they usually ate their meals. The solar was the most comfortable room in the castle, and the walls were often plastered and decorated. But it was drafty, because the windows had no glass in them.

The keep often contained a chapel, another bedroom, and an office as well.

▷During the mid-1100s, many stone keeps were built. This picture shows what one of these looked like inside. The bottom story was used to store food and other goods. The lord and his family lived in the upper two stories.

8

The walled enclosure

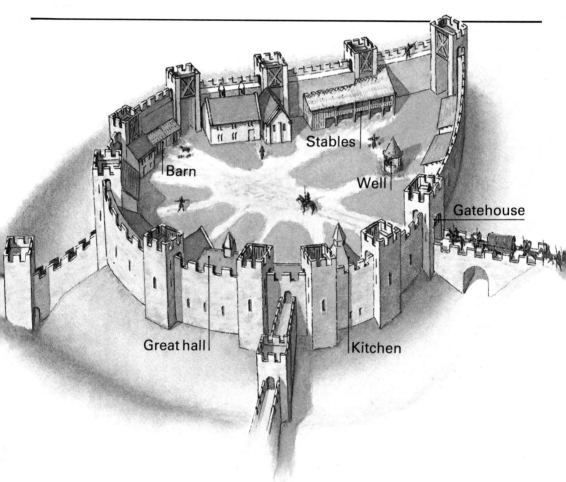

Barn

Stables

Well

Gatehouse

Great hall

Kitchen

△ Many towers protected the strong, high walls of this castle. If enemies fought their way into the bailey, they had to break into each tower before they could completely capture the castle.

This stone castle was built in the late 1100s. It had a stronger, higher wall with many more towers along it. The nobleman and his family no longer lived in a cramped keep. They had a large hall within the bailey.

The king and many of his noblemen owned more than one castle. These were often great distances apart, and the lord would spend part of the year in each one. A chief guard, known as the constable, was in charge of the castle while the lord was away.

Each castle also had a steward. He was usually informed in advance when the lord planned to visit the castle. The steward made sure that there was enough to eat, and that everyone had a place to sleep.

▽When a nobleman traveled from castle to castle, many people went with him. There were servants, ladies-in-waiting, entertainers, the whole family, and knights to guard them all. The lord carried most of his belongings with him in huge wagons.

11

Life in a castle

△ The kitchen was very hot and smelly, and liable to catch fire. So, it was often separate from the lord's home.

Here, meat is being cooked on a spit, while a stew bubbles in the cauldron. Bread was baked in the oven at the side of the fireplace. Meanwhile, birds had to be plucked, water fetched, fires built, and so on.

The castle buildings and weapons had to be kept in good repair in case of attack. The nobleman, his family, priests, knights, and often his guests, had to be fed and clothed. So, many servants were needed, including stable-hands, cooks, tailors and launderers. One of the most important was the keeper of the wardrobe. He looked after the lord's clothes and other goods.

12

▽ The armorer looked after the weapons and armor. He made sure that everyone had the right equipment to defend the castle. He also saw that it was in good condition – that the chain mail was free of rust, the swords were sharp and the crossbows were in working order.

The lady of the castle ensured that the household was well run. Her daughters were taught at home, but her sons were often sent to another castle. They learned good manners, how to shoot with a bow and arrow, and how to fight with a sword. They also had to be able to read and write, and understand Latin.

Castle amusements

Life in a castle was not all hard work. The lord and his family also had time to enjoy themselves. They played chess, checkers and dice, and read or sang.

Sometimes tournaments were held, in which groups of knights fought mock battles. This was good practice for warfare, as well as being fun.

People often went hunting with hounds for stag or boar. Another popular sport was falconry, in which birds of prey were trained to catch small animals.

▽ On special occasions, the lord would hold a banquet. In one meal his guests might have brawn made from a pig's head and jelly, pies, puddings, baked fish, roasted pork, venison, pheasants, and many other birds, such as larks and swans, which we do not eat today.

Attacking a castle

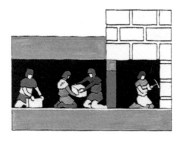

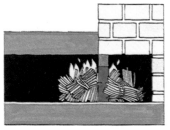

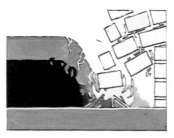

△ Soldiers dug under the wall, propping it up with wood. They then made a fire to burn the props. Part of the tower collapsed, and they could enter the castle. This is called undermining.

Although a castle could be a comfortable home, no one inside it could forget that it was also a fortress and might one day be attacked. Everyone hoped that the walls and gates were strong enough to keep the enemy out.

In those days there were no powerful explosives or guns. The attackers had to climb over the walls or try to knock them down. They could also prevent supplies from reaching the castle.

Soldiers used ladders and scaling towers to help them get over the walls and into the castle.

Several machines could be used to damage a castle. One was a battering ram, which was a strong tree trunk with an iron tip. Other machines, such as mangonels and trebuchets, could hurl heavy rocks at the walls or knock the corners off the towers. They were also used to throw missiles over the walls, smashing the buildings inside.

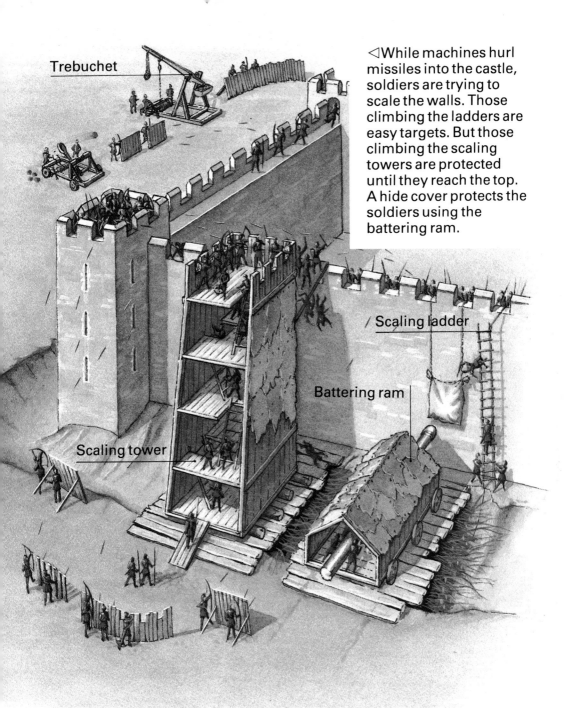

Trebuchet

◁While machines hurl missiles into the castle, soldiers are trying to scale the walls. Those climbing the ladders are easy targets. But those climbing the scaling towers are protected until they reach the top. A hide cover protects the soldiers using the battering ram.

Scaling ladder

Battering ram

Scaling tower

17

Under siege

Walkway

Hoards

Moat

Mangonel

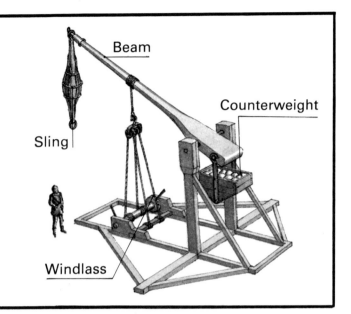

▷ The trebuchet was a huge catapult. It was used, for example, to break a castle's hourds.

A missile was placed in the sling. The beam could be wound down using a machine called a windlass. When released, the beam shot upright, pulled down by the counterweight. This hurled the missile out of the sling with great force.

Beam

Counterweight

Sling

Windlass

◁ This castle was easier to defend than the one on the previous page. It was surrounded by a moat, so the enemy could not undermine the walls. Missiles could knock the corners off square towers. But this castle had round towers, and so the missiles glanced off.

An attack or siege on a castle could last for weeks or months. During this time, no fresh food or water could reach the castle. When all the supplies had been used up, the castle had to surrender. So the people inside the castle fought back as hard as they could, hoping to drive the enemy away quickly or to be rescued.

They built wooden platforms, called hourds, out from the walls. These had slatted floors so that missiles could be dropped, and arrows fired down, on to the enemy.

19

The keep gatehouse

The design of castles continued to change. By the late 1200s, some castles were so strong that it was almost impossible for enemies to break in.

The weakest part of any castle was usually the gate. So its defenses were much improved. Visitors first had to pass through a strongly guarded outer gate, the barbican. The drawbridge had to be lowered before they could cross over the moat to the gatehouse. Here, the entrance was blocked by a huge iron-covered gate, called a port-cullis, set in grooves in the wall.

The gatehouse was as strong as a keep in an older castle. So, it is called a keep gatehouse. Soldiers could continue to defend it, even when the rest of the castle was overrun. Like a keep, the keep gatehouse was also a home – the home of the constable. The lord lived in a more comfortable building within the castle.

▷ The main room of the keep gatehouse was on the middle story. It contained winding devices to raise and lower the drawbridge and portcullises. If enemy soldiers tricked their way into the gate passage, they found themselves trapped between two portcullises. The room above had murder holes in the floor, through which arrows could be fired on them.

20

The concentric castle

A keep gatehouse guarded the entrance to a concentric castle. A concentric castle had two sets of walls, one inside the other.

A wide moat surrounded the castle. The lower, outer wall was sometimes strengthened with towers. Barbicans and gatehouses guarded the entrances. If enemy soldiers broke through this wall into the outer bailey, they were surrounded by archers. For within the outer bailey was a stronger, taller wall containing massive gatehouses and towers.

It was very difficult for an enemy army to break into and capture a con-centric castle. But the people in the castle could still be forced to surrender through hunger. Also, many of the defenders fought for the lord only because they were paid to. If the enemy paid them more, they sometimes let them in.

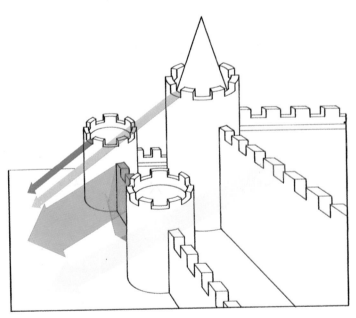

△ This is Beaumaris Castle in North Wales. Building work started in 1295 and continued on and off for nearly thirty years. Unfortunately, it was never finished. It was built for King Edward I of England, who was trying to conquer the Welsh.

◁ Soldiers on the higher, inner wall could fire over the heads of those on the lower, outer wall.

23

Building a castle

△ The masons built the stone walls and towers, while the carpenters made floors, doors and furniture. Many of their tools look familiar.

The big stone castles, particularly the huge concentric ones, often took more than ten years to complete. As many as 3,000 workers at a time might be employed on them.

First the site was chosen and the plans of the castle were drawn up. If there was no suitable stone in the area it had to be brought, sometimes over many miles. Carpenters, masons and other craftsmen, and laborers, were hired and supervised by the master mason. They sometimes traveled great distances, too, and needed a guard through hostile country.

▽ The castle builders erected scaffolding. Cranes and hoists were used to lift heavy materials. These were carried around the building by laborers.

The castle becomes a home

Gradually, times changed. The kings and lords who owned the castles no longer fought among themselves. There were fewer rebellions, and the owners of castles were no longer in danger from the people living around them. Wars were now fought by full-time soldiers in the king's army, not by knights and followers of the king's noblemen.

▽ Jousts were a popular entertainment. Here, one knight is using a lance to unseat his opponent. Unlike the tournaments of earlier times, jousts did not train people for battle.

For all these reasons, castles no longer had to be fortresses. They could be made more comfortable, by removing some of their defenses and putting in wide glass windows to let the light in. Or their owners could move out into large country houses.

People's lives began to change, too. Most of their time used to be spent preparing for battle. Now they were free to enjoy poetry, music, dance and other pleasures.

△ A nobleman no longer needed to live in a fortress. But he still wanted his home to look like a castle. This is Herstmonceux Castle in Sussex, England. It looks like a castle, but the defenses are just for show.

27

Castles today

▷Many castles were so well built that they would have lasted until today, but for gunpowder. Corfe in Dorset was an older type of castle with a tall, square keep. It was nearly destroyed by gunpowder in 1646, during the English Civil War.

Only a few castles are still used as homes. One of these is Windsor Castle, England, where Queen Elizabeth II lives for part of each year.

Most castles are now in ruins. Some have been rebuilt so that visitors can see what they looked like and imagine what it was like to live in them, hundreds of years ago. Often there is a small museum inside to help people learn more about the castle and its history. If you get the chance to visit a castle, you may spot some of the features shown in this book.

◁ Burg Eltz in Germany was built in the early 1100s. The wooden-framed buildings with pointed roofs were added in the 1400s. The castle has been restored, and still looks much like it did 500 years ago.

▽ Dover Castle was built during the 1180s by Henry II of England. It had a massive square keep surrounded by a curtain wall containing fourteen towers.

Glossary

Here is a list of some of the technical words used in this book.

Bailey
The area inside the castle walls.

Barbican
A small fortification at a castle entrance, in front of the gatehouse.

Concentric castle
A castle with two sets of walls, one inside the other.

Constable
The person in charge of the castle's defences.

▽ **Crenel**
Regular gap in a wall through which guards could look out.

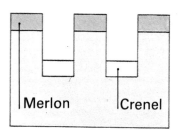

Crossbow
A mechanical bow for firing arrows.

Curtain wall
Stone wall surrounding the bailey

Drawbridge
A bridge over a moat or ditch, which could be drawn up.

Fortification
A structure which protects or defends.

Gatehouse
The fortified gateway to a castle, which was sometimes also a home.

Hoards
A platform built out from the castle walls.

Keep
A strong stone tower. It was the safest place in the castle, and was the lord's home.

Knight
A special kind of soldier on horseback, serving a nobleman or king.

Master mason
The person in charge of designing and building a stone castle.

Merlon
Stone between the crenels in a crenellated wall (*see diagram*).

Moat
A wide ditch, filled with water, surrounding a castle.

Motte
A mound of earth on which a tower was built. Wooden castles and some stone castles had mottes.

Portcullis
A metal-covered grating which could be raised and lowered from within the castle. It protected the entrance to a castle.

Solar
The private room of the lord and his family, within the castle.

Steward
The person in charge of the housekeeping in the castle.

Castle facts

Here are some interesting facts about castles.

Master James of St George was one of the most famous master masons. He built castles for King Edward I of England in the 1290s. The famous Welsh castles of Flint, Rhuddlan, Harlech, Beaumaris, Conway and Caernarvon were his work.

During a siege, an army sometimes used machines, such as the trebuchet, to hurl dead horses or even dead people into the castle they were attacking. They hoped that these would spread disease within the castle, making the defenders too ill to fight.

In the 1100s, many knights journeyed from Europe to the Middle East. Here they fought the Muslims for the Holy Land. These knights were called crusaders. They also built castles, and learned a lot about castle design.

▽This is Krak des Chevaliers in Syria. It is a concentric castle, and is one of the most famous of the crusader castles.

Index

armorer 13

bailey 4, 6, 7, 10, 22, 30
banquet 15
barbican 20, 22, 30
battering ram 16, 17
Beaumaris Castle 22, 23
builders 24, 25
Burg Eltz 29

chain mail 13
concentric castle 22, 23, 24, 30, 31
constable 11, 20, 30
Corfe Castle 28
crenel 6, 30
crusader 31
curtain wall 6, 30

Dover Castle 29
drawbridge 4, 7, 20, 21, 30

education 13
Edward I 31
Elizabeth II 28
English Civil War 28

falconry 15
food 12, 15
fortification 30

games 14, 15, 26
gatehouse 4, 6, 20, 22, 30

gate passage 20
great hall 7, 10
gunpowder 28

Henry II 29
Herstmonceux Castle 27
hoards 18, 19, 30
hunting 15

joust 26

keep 6, 7, 8, 28, 29, 30
keeper of the wardrobe 12
keep gatehouse 20, 21, 22
kitchen 12
knight 5, 11, 15, 26, 30
Krak des Chevaliers 31

ladder 16, 17
loophole 6, 7

mangonel 16
mason 24, 25
Master James 31
master mason 25, 30, 31
merlon 6, 30
moat 7, 19, 20, 22, 30
motte 5, 6, 30
motte-and-bailey castle 4–5
murder hole 20, 21

palisade 4
portcullis 20, 21, 30

scaling tower 16, 17
servant 12–13
siege 16, 17, 18, 19
solar 6
steward 11, 30
sword 13

tournament 15
trebuchet 16, 17, 19, 31

undermining 16

wagon 11
walkway 6, 7
walled enclosure 10–11
weapon 13, 16, 17, 18, 19
windlass 19
Windsor Castle 28
wooden castle 4–5, 6

32